EDGE BOOKS™

BLOODIEST BATTLES

AMERICA'S DEADLIEST DAY

THE BATTLE OF ANTIETAM

BY TERRI DOUGHERTY

CONSULTANT:
Tim Solie
Adjunct Professor of History
Minnesota State University, Mankato

Capstone press®

Mankato, Minnesota

Edge Books are published by Capstone Press,
151 Good Counsel Drive, P.O. Box 669, Mankato, Minnesota 56002.
www.capstonepress.com

Library of Congress Cataloging-in-Publication Data
Dougherty, Terri.
   America's deadliest day: the Battle of Antietam / by Terri Dougherty.
   p. cm. — (Edge books. Bloodiest battles)
   Includes bibliographical references and index.
   ISBN-13: 978-1-4296-1935-6 (hardcover)
   ISBN-10: 1-4296-1935-X (hardcover)
   1. Antietam, Battle of, Md., 1862 — Juvenile literature. I. Title. II. Series.
E474.65.D68 2009
973.7'336 — dc22   2008000532

Summary: Describes events before, during, and after the battle of Antietam,
including key players, weapons, and battle tactics.

Editorial Credits
Mandy Robbins, editor; Bob Lentz, designer/illustrator; Jo Miller,
      photo researcher

Photo Credits
Corbis/Schenectady Museum/Hall of Electrical History Foundation, 6, 7
Courtesy of the North Carolina Office of Archives and History, Raleigh,
      North Carolina, 12 (inset)
Getty Images Inc./MPI, 8 (right), 14, 16; Time Life Pictures/Buyenlarge/
      Buyenlarge, 8 (left); Time Life Pictures/NPS/Harpers Ferry National
      Historic Park, 12–13
©Jupiterimages Corporation, 15
National Park Service, cover (bottom); Alexander Gardner, cover (top), 4,
      18–19, 21, 24, 26; Keith Snyder, 29
Shutterstock/C. Kurt Holter, cover (middle)

1 2 3 4 5 6 13 12 11 10 09 08

TABLE OF CONTENTS

CHAPTER 1

THE BLOODIEST DAY

The battle of Antietam was fought in several locations along
Antietam Creek. One place was a sunken road now called Bloody Lane.

The battle of Antietam marked the bloodiest day America has ever seen. The sun was setting when the bullets stopped flying on September 17, 1862. The battle had raged since dawn. When the fighting ended, 12,400 Union soldiers and 10,320 Confederate soldiers were killed, wounded, missing, or captured.

North against South

The battle of Antietam took place during the Civil War (1861–1865). At that time, life in the northern United States was very different from life in the South. Most of the nation's factories were in the North. Immigrants from Europe found work in the factories. In the South, large farms called plantations used slave labor.

Many people in the North wanted to end slavery. But people in the southern states did not want to change their way of life. Eleven southern states chose to **secede** from the United States.

secede — to formally withdraw from a group or an organization

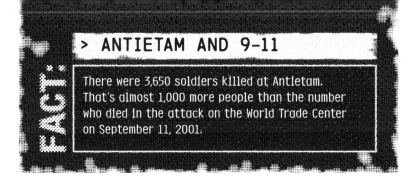

FACT:

> ANTIETAM AND 9-11

There were 3,650 soldiers killed at Antietam. That's almost 1,000 more people than the number who died in the attack on the World Trade Center on September 11, 2001.

The southern states formed the Confederate States of America, or the Confederacy. The Civil War began on April 12, 1861, when the Confederacy, also known as the South, attacked Fort Sumter.

Both sides fought for what they thought was right. The North, also called the Union, wanted to keep the United States together. Southerners wanted to govern themselves. More than 600,000 soldiers died while the nation was divided in war.

The Confederate States of America printed their own money.

Road to Antietam

When the war began, both sides thought it would be brief. They were wrong. The war raged for four years.

The South won some of the first battles. But the North captured several important riverside forts. The North also won the battle of Shiloh in Tennessee. The win gave the North control of much of the Mississippi River and the port at New Orleans.

The South hoped to bring France and England into the war on its side. These countries needed Southern cotton to keep their cloth factories running. But England and France wouldn't enter the war until they were sure the South could win. The South needed to prove its strength. Victory at Antietam would do just that.

CHAPTER 2

LEE AND McCLELLAN

General Lee (left) and General McClellan (right) had very different fighting styles.

In the beginning, the Union had more advantages than the South. The North had more money and an organized army. It had more railroads to move supplies for the army and more factories for building weapons.

General George B. McClellan led the Union Army. He was very popular with his men and skilled at organizing his soldiers. But McClellan had one main fault. He often hesitated to send all his troops into battle. McClellan did not act until he was sure he could win. He was so afraid to lose a battle, he often wasn't bold enough to win.

General Robert E. Lee led the Confederate Army. He had a smaller army but was not afraid to take chances. By late summer 1862, Lee wanted to move the fighting out of Virginia. He didn't want to fight on southern soil during the fall. Lee wanted to give southern farmers time to harvest their crops.

> CONFEDERATE HUNGER

Food was scarce during the Confederates' march to Maryland. Many Confederate soldiers knocked on the doors of homes in Maryland to ask for something to eat.

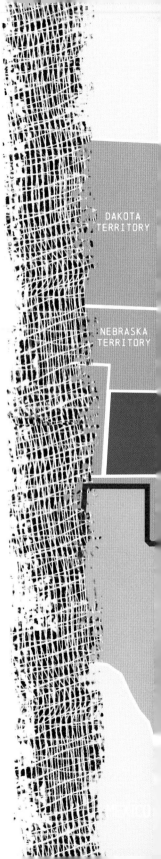

DAKOTA TERRITORY

NEBRASKA TERRITORY

In late August 1862, the South won an important victory at Bull Run in Virginia. The Confederate soldiers felt confident. Lee thought this was a good time to move into northern territory. He ordered his army to **invade** Maryland.

Lee's soldiers were very tired on the march to Maryland. Many of them had no shoes, little **ammunition**, and few supplies. They were also very hungry.

Some of the soldiers fell behind. They were called stragglers. Hundreds of stragglers reduced the size of Lee's army. The Confederate Army had, at most, 55,000 men by the time it reached Antietam Creek in Maryland. The North had a force of almost 90,000.

invade — to send armed forces into another country in order to take it over

ammunition — bullets and other objects that can be fired from weapons

Moving into Maryland

The Confederate Army marched into Maryland in early September 1862. Lee crossed the Potomac River near Leesburg, Virginia. The troops camped near Frederick, Maryland. There, Lee issued Special Order 191. In it, he told his officers where to go for the first attack in Maryland. Lee ordered his army to split up. One group of soldiers would attack Union soldiers at Harpers Ferry. The other group would move into Pennsylvania and take over the important railroad center of Harrisburg.

> SPECIAL ORDER 191

When he read Special Order 191, McClellan was reported to have said, "Here is a paper with which, if I cannot whip Bobby Lee, I will be willing to go home."

The North was not going to let Lee invade Maryland without a fight. McClellan and the Union Army followed Lee into Maryland. They came into Frederick a few days after the Confederates had left.

On September 13, a Union soldier found a copy of Lee's special order wrapped around three cigars. A Confederate soldier had accidentally left it there. McClellan read the order and immediately knew where Lee's troops were going to be.

Harpers Ferry was guarded by Union soldiers. For Lee to push farther north, his troops had to take control of the town.

McClellan could have attacked both groups of Confederates while their army was divided. For some unknown reason, he didn't. McClellan was cautious and left the next day. This gave the South time to defeat the Union soldiers at Harpers Ferry and take over the town.

The rest of Lee's army was in the town of Sharpsburg, Maryland. The Union Army marched toward them. They planned to crush the Confederates.

In September 1862, the citizens of the quiet town of Sharpsburg found themselves in the middle of a war zone.

The most popular Civil War weapon was the rifle. Many soldiers carried Springfield rifles. This rifle had a grooved barrel that was 39 inches (99 centimeters) long. The grooves cut into the inside of the barrel made the bullets rotate. Rotating bullets could fly farther than bullets shot from a gun with a smooth barrel. A rifle was also more accurate than a smoothbore gun. It could hit a target 500 yards (457 meters) away.

Some Union soldiers carried repeating rifles like the Spencer and the Henry rifles. These rifles could fire several shots in a row.

There were not enough rifles for all the soldiers, so some carried older smoothbore guns. These guns fired round lead balls. They could hit targets that were 70 to 100 yards (64 to 91 meters) away. Smoothbore guns were not as reliable as Springfield rifles. They often failed to fire.

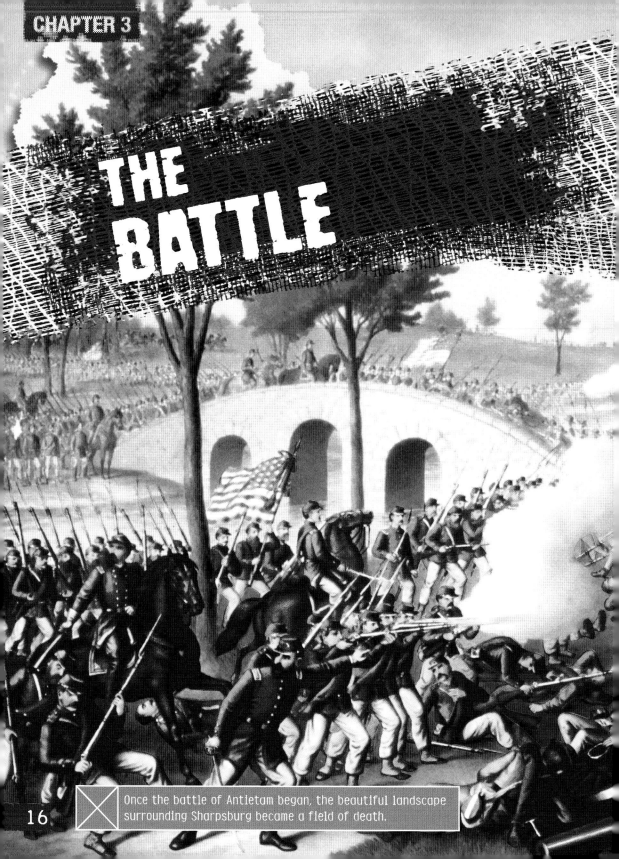

CHAPTER 3

THE BATTLE

Once the battle of Antietam began, the beautiful landscape surrounding Sharpsburg became a field of death.

Lee positioned the Confederate soldiers for battle in the hills near Sharpsburg. The hills had woods and rock ledges where Lee's soldiers could hide. The Union soldiers would have to move across open ground when they attacked.

The Union soldiers marched to the banks of Antietam Creek, near Sharpsburg. McClellan planned to attack the **flanks** of Lee's army and then the center. The anxious troops waited for sunrise, when the battle would begin.

Attack!

The boom of artillery shattered the silence on the morning of September 17. Northern troops aimed their cannons at the left flank of Lee's army. They marched shoulder to shoulder toward the Confederate Army like a wall of men. But they didn't know that Confederate soldiers were waiting for them in a nearby cornfield.

flanks — the far left and right sides of a group of soldiers

The Confederate soldiers rose from the cornfield and fired. The Union wall crumbled. Men fell dead in rows.

The battle was just beginning. The roar of cannon fire echoed as the Confederates charged, and Union soldiers charged back. By 9:00 in the morning, the corn was flattened. Bodies of dead and wounded soldiers blanketed the ground.

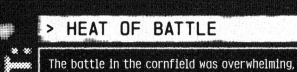

> HEAT OF BATTLE

The battle in the cornfield was overwhelming, even for seasoned soldiers. One surviving soldier said the battle was so intense that the lines of soldiers "melted away like wax."

The bodies of the dead lay on the ground for days before they could be buried.

The North attacked again near Dunker Church. Union soldiers charged at the Confederate line and almost broke through. But a fierce Confederate rally stopped them from gaining any ground.

The fighting near the church continued for hours. During one Union push forward, some Confederate soldiers ran toward the woods. But they had to climb over a fence to reach the woods. Many were shot down before they could make it to the other side.

An Ambush

South of the cornfield, Union General John Sedgwick led his soldiers into the West Woods. The Confederate Army had already snuck into that area. They waited quietly while the Union soldiers advanced. When they had the Union soldiers nearly surrounded, the Confederates attacked. Bullets flew at the Union soldiers from all sides. In 20 minutes, nearly 2,500 men lay killed or wounded.

Although many men lost their lives during the fight by Dunker Church, neither side claimed victory.

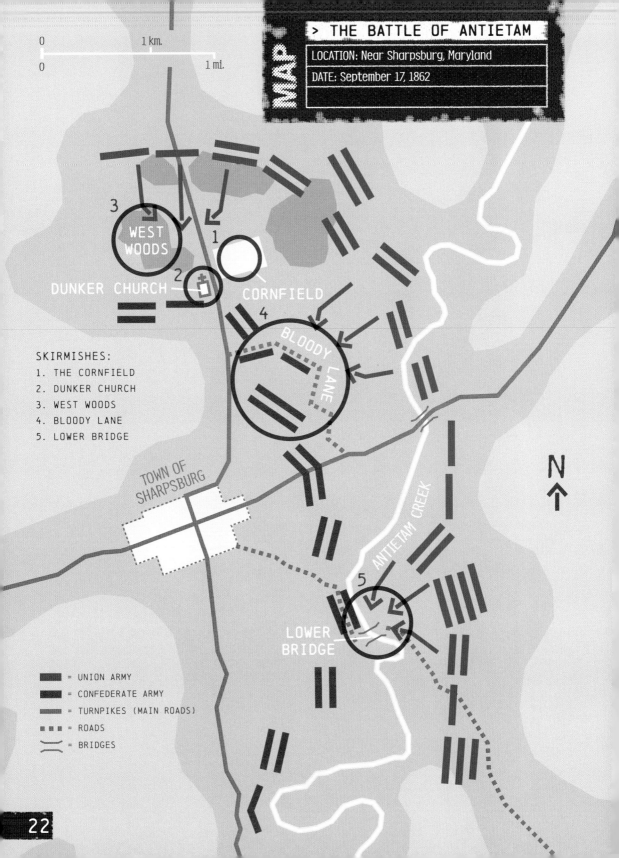

> # THE BATTLE OF ANTIETAM

MAP

LOCATION: Near Sharpsburg, Maryland

DATE: September 17, 1862

0 ——— 1 km.

0 ——— 1 mi.

WEST WOODS 3

1

DUNKER CHURCH 2

CORNFIELD

4

BLOODY LANE

SKIRMISHES:
1. THE CORNFIELD
2. DUNKER CHURCH
3. WEST WOODS
4. BLOODY LANE
5. LOWER BRIDGE

TOWN OF SHARPSBURG

ANTIETAM CREEK

N

5

LOWER BRIDGE

▬▬ = UNION ARMY
▬▬ = CONFEDERATE ARMY
▬▬ = TURNPIKES (MAIN ROADS)
▪▪▪ = ROADS
〰 = BRIDGES

Bloody Lane

Late in the morning, another Union **division** marched south to secure a dirt road. The Confederates were waiting along the banks of the road. Rifle fire rang out as the Confederates hammered the Union soldiers.

The troops fought for almost four hours. The Confederates finally retreated when a Union division made it around the side of its line.

After the Confederates fled, bodies of soldiers littered the road and the banks along it. To this day, that road is called Bloody Lane.

The Lower Bridge

The Union attacked the right flank of the Confederate Army in the afternoon. The Union then tried to cross Antietam Creek at the Lower Bridge. As the Union soldiers charged across the bridge, Confederate sharpshooters pelted them with bullets. Some Union soldiers managed to cross the bridge. Others walked across the creek in shallow water. Together, these soldiers moved toward Sharpsburg to cut off the Confederates' route of retreat.

division — a military unit made up of several smaller units called regiments

The Union Army could win if it succeeded in cutting off Lee's route of retreat. But at 4:00 in the afternoon, another Confederate division arrived from Harpers Ferry. The attack surprised the Union. Union soldiers retreated across Antietam Creek, failing to cut off Lee's route of retreat.

After the battle was over, survivors were left with the awful job of burying the dead.

The Union retreat marked the end of the fighting. It was a draw. The Union Army could not break the Confederate Army. The Confederates could not get any farther north.

McClellan Holds Back

McClellan could have attacked the Confederates again, but he wanted to get more troops first. He thought the South had many more men than they actually did. Lee had led his men wisely in this battle. The Union forces had attacked different places at different times. Lee moved his troops wherever they were needed. If all the Union forces had attacked at the same time, the Confederate Army could have quickly been defeated.

Retreat from the North

The Confederate Army did not wait for the Union to regroup. Lee's men were tired. The South did not have enough troops for another strike. The night of September 18, Lee and his soldiers returned to Virginia.

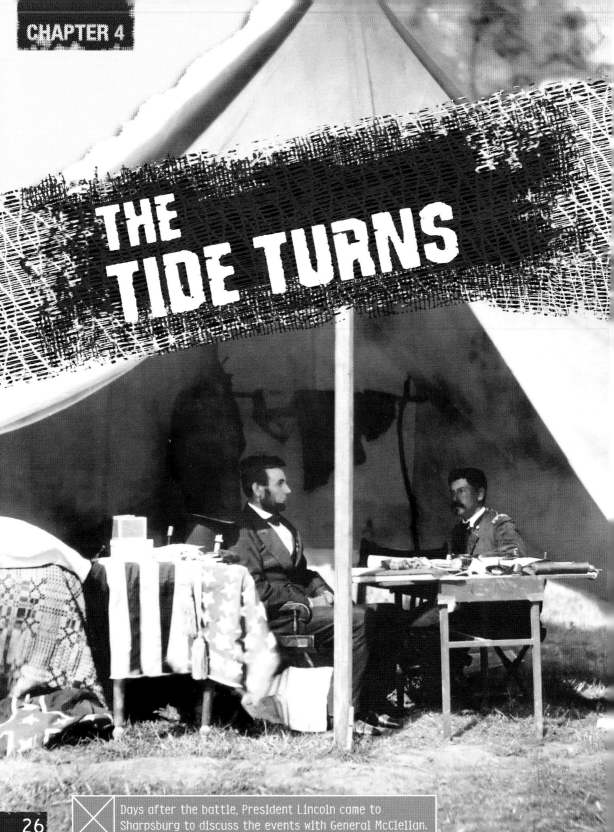

CHAPTER 4

THE TIDE TURNS

Days after the battle, President Lincoln came to Sharpsburg to discuss the events with General McClellan.

It could be argued that neither side won the battle of Antietam. But because the South retreated, the North claimed victory. England and France decided to stay out of the war. They were not sure the South could defeat the North. The Confederate Army's spirit was wounded after Antietam. The Union's hope was revived.

The Union victory was not complete, however. After the battle of Antietam, President Abraham Lincoln wanted McClellan to follow Lee and crush his army. McClellan refused. He said he needed more men, horses, and equipment. Lincoln grew tired of waiting for McClellan to attack. In November 1862, he removed McClellan from his position.

Emancipation Proclamation

Lincoln had been waiting for a Union victory to make an announcement. After Antietam, Lincoln announced the Emancipation Proclamation. This order freed the slaves in the Confederate states.

It took two more years of fighting before the war was over. On April 9, 1865, Lee surrendered to Union General Ulysses S. Grant. The nation was united, but bitterness over the war would linger for many years.

> ANTIETAM TODAY

Today, the area where the North and South clashed in Maryland is called Antietam National Battlefield. The bridge the Union soldiers crossed still stands. Thousands of men who died in the battle of Antietam are buried in a national cemetery at Sharpsburg.

At the park's visitor center, people can learn more about the battle of Antietam. The park helps visitors remember and honor the men who fought and died there.

The Confederates destroyed the Mumma family's farm during the battle of Antietam. This small family cemetery is all that remains.

GLOSSARY

ammunition (am-yuh-NI-shuhn) — bullets and other objects that can be fired from weapons

artillery (ar-TI-luhr-ee) — cannons and other large guns used during battles

division (duh-VI-zhuhn) — a military unit made up of several smaller units called regiments

flank (FLANGK) — the far left or right side of a group of soldiers, a fort, or a naval fleet

invade (in-VADE) — to send armed forces into another country or territory in order to take it over

plantation (plan-TAY-shuhn) — a large farm found in warm areas; before the Civil War, plantations in the South used slave labor.

retreat (ri-TREET) — to move back or withdraw from a difficult situation

rifle (RYE-fuhl) — a gun that is fired from the shoulder and has grooves in the barrel to make bullets travel farther

secede (si-SEED) — to formally withdraw from a group or an organization, often to form another organization

DeFord, Deborah H. *The Civil War*. Wars That Changed American History. Milwaukee: World Almanac Library, 2007.

Hama, Larry. *The Battle of Antietam: "The Bloodiest Day of Battle."* Graphic Battles of the Civil War. New York: Rosen, 2007.

Mattern, Joanne. *The Big Book of the Civil War*. Philadelphia: Courage Books, 2007.

INTERNET SITES

FactHound offers a safe, fun way to find Internet sites related to this book. All of the sites on FactHound have been researched by our staff.

Here's how:
1. Visit *www.facthound.com*
2. Choose your grade level.
3. Type in this book ID **142961935X** for age-appropriate sites. You may also browse subjects by clicking on letters, or by clicking on pictures and words.
4. Click on the **Fetch It** button.

FactHound will fetch the best sites for you!

INDEX